101 RECIPES WITH CHEESE

2895

$6

Item #3723
Made in USA

ISBN-13: 978-1-56383-27
ISBN-10: 1-56383-272-0

Y0-DKN-463

Gifts Like Nothing Else
(336)883-6264 or (336)882-0542

● 101 RECIPES WITH CHEESE

CHEESE
Cookbook

Copyright © 2007 CQ Products
Waverly, IA 50677
All rights reserved.
No part of this book may be reproduced or transmitted in any form or by any means, electronic or mechanical, including photocopying, recording or by any information storage and retrieval system, without permission in writing from the publisher, CQ Products.

Printed in the USA by G&R Publishing Co., Waverly, IA

Published and distributed by:

507 Industrial Street
Waverly, IA 50677

ISBN-13: 978-1-56383-272-7
ISBN-10: 1-56383-272-0
Item #3723

Appetizers

Pesto and Parmesan Pita Wedges

1 whole pita bread
3 T. prepared pesto

3 T. grated Parmesan cheese

Preheat the oven to 350°. Split pita bread into 2 rounds. Spread each pita round with pesto and sprinkle Parmesan cheese over top. Cut pitas into 6 wedges each. Place on an ungreased baking sheet. Bake in the oven for 10 to 12 minutes or until crisp. Serve pitas warm. Makes 12 pieces.

Parmesan Romano Bread

1 (1 lb.) loaf unsliced white bread
1 C. grated Parmesan cheese
1 C. grated Romano cheese
6 cloves garlic, minced
½ C. chopped fresh parsley
1 C. extra virgin olive oil, divided
2 T. dried red chile peppers

Preheat the oven to 300°. Place the unsliced white bread on a large oven-safe serving dish. Cut the loaf into 8 slices only halfway through. Carefully hold the slices open to sprinkle Parmesan cheese, Romano cheese, garlic, parsley and ½ cup extra virgin olive oil over the loaf. Spread dried red chile peppers around base of bread. Bake in the oven for 15 minutes, or until the cheese is melted but not browned. Remove from oven and drizzle with remaining olive oil. Serve bread warm. Makes 8 pieces.

Cheesy Sausage Balls

8 oz. pork sausage
1 (16 oz.) pkg. shredded
    Cheddar cheese
1 C. butter or margarine, softened

2 C. flour
½ tsp. salt
½ tsp. pepper

Preheat the oven to 400°. In a medium skillet over medium-high heat, cook the pork sausage until browned. Drain grease from skillet and set aside. In large bowl, combine shredded Cheddar cheese, butter, flour, salt and pepper. Beat with an electric mixer on medium-low speed. Stir in cooked pork sausage. Form the dough into 15 to 20 balls, each about 1″ in diameter and place on a baking sheet. Bake in the oven for 15 to 20 minutes or until golden brown. Serve sausage balls warm or cold. Makes 15 to 20 pieces.

Garlic and Parmesan Zucchini Bites

4 C. grated zucchini
1¾ C. biscuit baking mix
¾ C. grated Parmesan cheese
1 C. shredded sharp Cheddar cheese
4 eggs, beaten
½ C. vegetable oil

1 large onion, minced
4 cloves garlic, chopped
3 T. dried parsley
½ tsp. salt
¾ tsp. dried oregano

Preheat the oven to 400°. In a large bowl, combine the grated zucchini, biscuit mix, grated Parmesan cheese, shredded sharp Cheddar cheese, eggs, vegetable oil, minced onion, chopped garlic, dried parsley, salt and oregano. Spread the mixture into a greased 9 x 13″ baking pan. Bake in the oven for 25 to 30 minutes or until golden brown. Allow the mixture to cool. Cut into small squares to serve. Makes 18 pieces.

Stuffed Sausage Mushrooms

24 fresh large mushrooms
1 lb. Italian sausage
½ C. chopped green onions

1 C. spaghetti sauce
1 C. shredded mozzarella cheese

Preheat the oven to 350°. Remove stems from mushrooms and set caps aside. Chop the mushroom stems and set aside. In a medium skillet over medium-high heat, cook sausage until browned. Remove sausage from skillet with a slotted spoon. In the same skillet, sauté chopped green onions and mushroom stems. Stir in spaghetti sauce and cooked sausage. Stuff sausage mixture into mushroom caps. Sprinkle mozzarella cheese over top of the stuffed mushrooms and place in a 10 x 15″ baking pan. Bake in the oven for 12 to 15 minutes or until cheese is melted. Serve stuffed mushrooms warm. Makes 24 pieces.

Tortellini Bites

½ C. fat-free milk
3 T. nonfat dry milk powder
1½ C. cottage cheese
¼ C. grated Parmesan cheese
1 T. lemon juice
1½ tsp. minced fresh rosemary
¼ tsp. salt
⅛ tsp. pepper
1 (9 oz.) pkg. refrigerated cheese tortellini

In a blender or food processor, blend together milk and non-fat milk powder. Add the cottage cheese, Parmesan cheese, lemon juice, rosemary, salt and pepper to the blender, cover and process until smooth. Cover mixture and chill in the refrigerator for 30 minutes. Bring a pot of lightly salted water to a boil. Add tortellini and cook until tender. Drain water from pot. Serve tortellini with chilled Parmesan sauce for dipping. Makes 3 cups of dip.

Cheesy Egg Salad Spread

2 C. shredded processed cheese
4 hard-cooked eggs, peeled and chopped
½ C. mayonnaise
¼ C. sweet pickle relish
1 tsp. mustard
Salt and pepper to taste

In a medium bowl, combine shredded processed cheese, hard-cooked eggs, mayonnaise, sweet pickle relish, mustard, salt and pepper; mix well. To serve, spread over crackers. Makes 3½ cups.

Cheddar Olive Squares

1 (16 oz.) pkg. hot roll mix
2 eggs, beaten separately
⅓ C. plus ¼ C. butter, melted
3 C. shredded Cheddar cheese, divided

1 T. poppy seeds
1 C. sliced stuffed green olives
1 T. minced onion
1 tsp. Worcestershire sauce

Preheat the oven to 400°. In a large bowl, dissolve yeast from hot roll mix in ¾ cup of warm water. Add 1 egg, ¼ cup melted butter, 1 cup shredded Cheddar cheese and poppy seeds. Add flour from hot roll mix and stir well. Press mixture into the bottom of a greased 10 x 15″ baking pan. Cover dough and let rise in a warm place for 45 minutes or until doubled. In a medium bowl, mix together remaining 2 cups of shredded Cheddar cheese, sliced stuffed olives, remaining egg, ⅓ cup butter, minced onion and Worcestershire sauce. Spread mixture over dough. Bake in the oven for 20 to 25 minutes or until golden brown. Cut bread into squares and serve warm. Makes 16 to 18 pieces.

Blue Cheese Pizza

1 (1 lb.) loaf frozen bread dough, thawed
3 T. olive oil
2 tsp. dried basil
2 tsp. dried oregano
1 tsp. garlic powder

1 small red onion, thinly sliced
2 plum tomatoes, chopped
1 C. shredded mozzarella cheese, divided
3 oz. crumbled blue cheese
2 T. grated Parmesan cheese

Preheat the oven to 425°. Press the frozen bread dough into the bottom of a greased 12″ pizza pan. Using a fork, prick dough several times. Cover and let rise 30 minutes. Brush the olive oil over the dough. In a small bowl, combine the dried basil, dried oregano and garlic powder; sprinkle over dough. Bake in the oven for 10 minutes. Remove from oven and arrange sliced onion and chopped tomatoes over crust. Sprinkle the shredded mozzarella cheese, crumbled blue cheese and Parmesan cheese over top. Bake 8 to 10 minutes longer or until golden brown. To serve, slice into wedges or squares. Makes 10 to 12 pieces.

Swiss and Onion on Rye

1 (2.8 oz.) can French-fried onions, crushed
¾ C. cooked crumbled bacon
½ C. mayonnaise

3 C. shredded Swiss cheese
1 (14 oz.) jar pizza sauce
1 (16 oz.) pkg. snack rye bread, sliced

Preheat the oven to 350°. In a medium bowl, combine the crushed French-fried onions, crumbled cooked bacon, salad dressing and shredded Swiss cheese. Spread 1 teaspoon of pizza sauce over each slice of rye bread. Top pizza sauce with 1 tablespoon of the Swiss cheese mixture. Place bread slices in a single layer on a baking sheet. Bake in the oven for 12 to 14 minutes or until cheese is melted. Let cool slightly before serving. Makes 40 to 44 pieces.

Blue Cheese Bread Bites

¼ C. butter
½ C. blue cheese

1 (11 oz.) tube refrigerated breadsticks

Preheat the oven to 400°. In a small saucepan over medium heat, melt the butter and blue cheese. Unroll the tube of refrigerated breadsticks and cut each stick into 4 pieces. Place the breadsticks in a foil-lined jelly roll pan. Pour blue cheese mixture over dough. Bake in the oven for 20 minutes or until butter is absorbed and rolls are lightly browned. Serve bread bites warm. Makes 48 pieces.

Two-Cheese Zucchini Squares

½ C. grated Parmesan cheese, divided
½ C. vegetable oil, divided
½ C. sesame seeds
1 onion, chopped
1 clove garlic, minced
2½ C. grated zucchini
6 eggs, beaten
⅓ C. dried bread crumbs
½ tsp. salt
½ tsp. dried basil
½ tsp. dried oregano
¼ tsp. pepper
3 C. shredded Cheddar cheese

Preheat the oven to 325°. Sprinkle 3 tablespoons of Parmesan cheese over a greased 9 x 13″ baking pan. In a medium skillet over medium high heat, warm ½ tablespoon vegetable oil. Add sesame seeds and cook until lightly browned; set aside. In a large bowl, combine remaining vegetable oil, chopped onion, minced garlic, grated zucchini, eggs, dried bread crumbs, salt, dried basil, dried oregano, pepper and shredded Cheddar cheese. Press mixture into baking pan. Sprinkle remaining Parmesan cheese and reserved sesame seeds over the zucchini mixture. Bake in the oven 30 minutes. Let cool at least 15 minutes before cutting into 1″ squares to serve. Makes 18 to 20 pieces.

Leek Tarts

1 (2 count) pkg. 9″ refrigerated
  pie crust dough
4 oz. provolone cheese, shredded
1 lb. leeks, white portion only, sliced
6 medium plum tomatoes, thinly sliced

¼ C. grated Parmesan cheese
1½ tsp. garlic powder
⅛ tsp. pepper
1 C. shredded mozzarella cheese

Preheat the oven to 425°. Place each sheet of refrigerated pie crust dough on a greased baking sheet. Sprinkle shredded provolone cheese over each sheet, leaving 1″ exposed around the edges. Arrange sliced leeks and tomato slices over shredded provolone cheese. Sprinkle Parmesan cheese, garlic powder and pepper over the top of tomatoes and leeks. Top with shredded mozzarella cheese. Fold exposed edges partway over the filling. Bake in the oven for 18 to 22 minutes or until crusts are lightly browned. To serve, cut each tart into 6 to 8 wedges. Makes 12 to 16 pieces.

Pepperoni Provolone Pizza Swirls

1 (10 oz.) can refrigerated pizza crust dough
¼ lb. Genoa salami, sliced
¼ lb. pepperoni sausage, sliced
¼ lb. provolone cheese, sliced
½ C. shredded mozzarella cheese

Preheat the oven to 350°. Roll pizza crust dough into a 10 x 14″ rectangle on a greased baking sheet. Layer the crust with sliced Genoa salami, sliced pepperoni and sliced provolone cheese. Sprinkle with mozzarella cheese leaving ½″ exposed around the edges. Roll up the crust and seal the edges using a fork. Bake in the oven for 25 minutes or until golden brown. To serve, slice into 1″ pieces. Makes 4 to 6 pieces.

Mini Ham and Cheese Quiches

½ C. butter
1 (5 oz.) container processed sharp Cheddar cheese spread
1 C. flour
1 egg
½ C. milk
¼ tsp. salt
½ C. finely chopped ham
½ C. shredded Monterey Jack cheese

Preheat the oven to 350°. In a small bowl, cut butter and processed cheese spread into flour until well blended. Add 2 tablespoons of water and toss with a fork until a ball forms. Chill in the refrigerator for 1 hour. Press 1 tablespoon of the mixture onto the bottom and up the sides of greased miniature muffin cups. In a small bowl, beat together the egg, milk and salt. Stir in chopped ham and shredded Monterey Jack cheese. Spoon 1 teaspoon of the mixture into each shell. Bake in the oven for 30 minutes or until golden brown. Let stand for 5 minutes before serving. Makes 12 mini quiches.

Four-Cheese Stuffed Bread

- 1 (1 lb.) loaf French bread
- 2 C. diced tomatoes
- 1 C. shredded mozzarella cheese
- 1 C. shredded Cheddar cheese
- 1 medium onion, minced
- ¼ C. grated Romano cheese
- ¼ C. chopped ripe olives
- ¼ C. Italian salad dressing
- 1 tsp. chopped fresh basil
- 1 tsp. chopped fresh oregano

Preheat the oven to 350°. Cut off the top half of the French bread loaf and set aside. Hollow out the bottom of the loaf, leaving a ½″ shell. Discard or store the unused bread pieces. In a medium bowl, combine the diced tomatoes, shredded mozzarella cheese, shredded Cheddar cheese, minced onion, grated Romano cheese, chopped olives, Italian salad dressing, chopped fresh basil and chopped fresh oregano. Spoon the mixture into the hollowed out loaf and replace the top. Wrap the stuffed French bread loaf in foil and bake in the oven for 25 minutes or until cheese is melted. Slice the loaf into 1″ pieces and serve warm. Makes 10 to 12 pieces.

Sunshine Cheese Crisps

2 C. shredded Cheddar cheese
½ C. grated Parmesan cheese
½ C. butter, softened
1 C. flour
¼ tsp. salt
1 C. quick-cooking oats
⅔ C. salted sunflower kernels

Preheat the oven to 400°. In a medium bowl, combine shredded Cheddar cheese, grated Parmesan cheese, butter and 3 tablespoons of water. In a small bowl, mix together flour and salt; add to cheese mixture. Stir in oats and sunflower seeds. Knead the dough until it holds together; shape into a 12″ roll. Cover the roll with plastic wrap and chill in the refrigerator for 4 hours. Remove roll from refrigerator and let stand 10 minutes at room temperature. Cut roll into ⅛″ slices. Place the slices on a greased foil-lined baking sheet. Bake in the oven for 10 minutes or until edges are golden. Let cheese crisps cool before serving. Makes 30 to 32 pieces.

Red Potato Nachos

8 medium red potatoes
1 (1 oz.) pkg. ranch-style salad dressing mix
1 (12 oz.) jar pickled jalapeno pepper slices, drained
2 C. shredded Cheddar cheese
2 C. shredded Monterey Jack cheese
2 C. sour cream
6 green onions, chopped

Preheat the oven to 350°. Bring a pot of lightly salted water to a boil. Place the red potatoes in the pot and return the water to a boil. Reduce heat, cover and cook for 15 to 20 minutes or until tender. Drain water from pot and let cool. Cut potatoes into ¼" thick slices and place, in a single layer, in greased 10 x 15" baking pans. Sprinkle each potato with some of the ranch-style salad dressing mix, one jalapeno slice, shredded Cheddar cheese and shredded Monterey Jack cheese. Bake in the oven for 10 to 12 minutes or until cheese is melted. To serve, top potato slices with sour cream and green onions. Makes 20 to 24 pieces.

Herbed Cheese Spread

1 (12 oz.) container cream cheese, softened
½ (4 oz.) pkg. crumbled feta cheese
¼ (4 oz.) pkg. crumbled blue cheese
½ tsp. dried basil
½ tsp. dried rosemary
1 T. chopped green onions
Apple slices or crackers, optional

In a medium bowl, stir together cream cheese, crumbled feta cheese, crumble blue cheese, dried basil, dried rosemary and chopped green onions. Serve with apple slices or crackers for dipping. Makes 3 cups.

Cheddar-Jack Cheese Bread

1 (8 oz.) loaf French bread
1 C. shredded Monterey Jack cheese
1 C. shredded Cheddar cheese
1 C. mayonnaise
3 green onions, chopped

Preheat the oven to 350°. Slice the French bread loaf in half lengthwise and remove the top of the loaf. In a large bowl, mix together the shredded Monterey Jack cheese, shredded Cheddar cheese, mayonnaise and chopped green onions. Spread the cheese mixture over the bottom and top halves of the bread. Place the bread halves on a baking sheet and bake in the oven for 15 minutes or until cheese is melted. Cut each half into 3 to 4 pieces. Serve cheese bread warm. Makes 6 to 8 pieces.

Blue Cheese Walnut Spread

1 (8 oz.) pkg. cream cheese, softened
1 (4 oz.) pkg. crumbled blue cheese
½ C. sour cream
½ tsp. Worcestershire sauce
½ C. chopped walnuts
2 T. chopped green onions
Crackers, French bread, fruits and vegetables for dipping, optional

In a large bowl, combine cream cheese, crumbled blue cheese, sour cream and Worcestershire sauce. Stir in walnuts and green onions. Cover and chill in the refrigerator for 1 hour. Serve spread with an assortment of crackers, French bread, fruit and vegetables. Makes 2½ cups.

Spicy Cheese Wafers

1 C. butter, softened
3 C. flour
1 (16 oz.) bag shredded
   Cheddar cheese

½ tsp. salt
½ tsp. dry mustard
½ tsp. cayenne pepper

Preheat the oven to 350°. In a medium bowl, mix together butter, flour, shredded Cheddar cheese, salt, dry mustard and cayenne pepper. Form mixture into 48 balls about ½″ in diameter and place on a baking sheet. Press balls with a fork to flatten. Bake in the oven for 15 minutes. Let cool before serving. Makes 48 pieces.

Parmesan and Prosciutto Pinwheels

1 (17.5 oz.) pkg. frozen puff pastry sheets, thawed
2 tsp. Dijon mustard
5 oz. prosciutto, thinly sliced
5 oz. Parmesan cheese, thinly sliced

Preheat the oven to 350°. Roll the thawed pastry out onto a flat surface. Spread Dijon mustard over the pastry sheets. Cover pastry sheets with a layer of sliced prosciutto. Cover the prosciutto with a layer of sliced Parmesan cheese. Beginning at the long side, roll up the pastry sheets. Cut into 8 pieces about 1″ thick each. Arrange the sections on a greased baking sheet and bake in the oven for 10 to 12 minutes. Let cool before serving. Makes 16 pieces.

Cheddar Cheesy Bacon Spread

10 slices bacon
2 C. shredded Cheddar cheese
1 T. grated onion

1 C. mayonnaise
Crackers for dipping, optional

In a medium skillet over medium-high heat, cook bacon until crisp and brown. Drain and crumble. In a medium bowl, mix together crumbled bacon, Cheddar cheese, grated onion and mayonnaise. Chill in the refrigerator for 1 hour. Serve with crackers for dipping or spreading. Makes 3 cups.

Asiago Cheese Toast

1 C. grated Asiago cheese
1 tsp. pressed garlic
⅓ C. mayonnaise
1 tsp. dried oregano
1 tsp. dried thyme
1 tsp. dried parsley
Pinch of salt
Pinch of pepper
1 French baguette, thinly sliced

Preheat the broiler. In a medium bowl, combine grated Asiago cheese, pressed garlic, mayonnaise, dried oregano, dried thyme, dried parsley, salt and pepper. Arrange the baguette pieces on a baking sheet. Spread the Asiago cheese mixture over the bread slices. Broil for 3 minutes, or until the cheese is melted and lightly browned. Remove from oven and serve immediately. Makes 10 to 12 pieces.

Baked Onion Spread

2 C. mayonnaise
2 C. chopped sweet onion

2 C. shredded Parmesan cheese
Crackers for dipping and spreading, optional

Preheat the oven to 350°. In large bowl, combine mayonnaise, chopped onions and shredded Parmesan cheese. Transfer mixture into a greased 2-quart baking dish. Bake in the oven for 45 minutes or until the top is slightly brown. Serve hot with butter crackers for dipping or spreading. Makes 6 cups.

Breakfast and Brunch

Muenster Spinach Quiche

12 oz. sliced Muenster cheese, divided
2 (10 oz.) pkgs. frozen chopped spinach, thawed and drained
2 eggs
⅓ C. grated Parmesan cheese
1 (8 oz.) pkg. cream cheese, softened
Salt and pepper to taste
Garlic powder to taste

Preheat the oven to 350°. Line a 9″ pie pan with 8 ounces of Muenster cheese slices. Press water out of spinach and place it in a large bowl. Mix in eggs, grated Parmesan cheese, cream cheese, salt, pepper and garlic powder. Spoon mixture into pie pan and top with remaining 4 ounces of sliced Muenster cheese. Bake in the oven for 35 minutes. Remove from oven and allow 10 minutes for casserole to set-up. To serve, slice quiche into wedges and place on individual serving plates. Makes 8 servings.

Mexican Egg Bake

- 6 (6″) tortillas
- 12 eggs
- ½ C. milk
- 1 C. shredded Cheddar cheese
- 1 C. shredded Monterey Jack cheese
- ¼ C. chopped red bell pepper
- 1 (4 oz.) can diced green chilies, drained
- 1 T. vegetable oil
- 1¼ C. sliced fresh mushrooms
- ½ medium green bell pepper, cut into 1″ strips
- 1 (10 oz.) can enchilada sauce

Preheat the oven to 350°. Layer tortillas in bottom of a greased 9 x 13″ baking pan so the edges overlap. In a large bowl, beat together eggs and milk. Stir in shredded Cheddar cheese, shredded Monterey Jack cheese, chopped red bell pepper and diced green chilies. Pour mixture over tortillas. Bake in the oven for 25 to 35 minutes or until eggs are set. In a medium skillet over medium-high heat, warm vegetable oil. Add sliced mushrooms and green bell pepper; cook until tender. Stir in enchilada sauce and cook until heated throughout. Spoon enchilada sauce mixture over baked eggs and serve. Makes 10 servings.

Bagel and Cheese Bake

½ lb. bacon, diced
½ C. chopped onion
3 plain bagels
1 C. shredded sharp Cheddar cheese
12 eggs, beaten

2 C. milk
2 tsp. chopped fresh parsley
¼ tsp. pepper
½ C. grated Parmesan cheese

In a medium skillet over medium-high heat, cook the bacon and onion until bacon is browned and onion is tender. Cut each bagel into 4 thin slices. Arrange 6 of the bagel slices in the bottom of a greased 9 x 13″ baking dish. Cover with the bacon and onion mixture and sprinkle the shredded Cheddar cheese over top. Place remaining 6 bagel slices on top of the cheese. In a medium bowl, whisk together the eggs, milk, chopped fresh parsley and pepper. Pour the egg mixture over the bagel layers. Cover and chill in the refrigerator for 8 hours. Preheat the oven to 400°. Remove the baking dish from the refrigerator and uncover. Bake in the oven for 25 to 30 minutes or until eggs are set. Sprinkle with Parmesan cheese and serve warm. Makes 10 to 12 servings.

Swiss and Sausage Quiche

½ lb. ground pork sausage
5 eggs
1 C. small curd cottage cheese
1 C. shredded Cheddar cheese

1 C. shredded Swiss cheese
¼ C. flour
½ tsp. baking powder

Preheat the oven to 350°. In a medium skillet over medium-high heat, cook sausage until browned. Drain grease from skillet, crumble sausage and set aside. In a medium bowl, beat the eggs. Add the sausage, cottage cheese, shredded Cheddar cheese, shredded Swiss cheese, flour and baking powder; mix well. Pour mixture into a greased 9″ square baking dish. Bake in the oven, uncovered, for 35 to 40 minutes or until eggs are set. Let stand for 5 minutes before serving. Makes 6 to 8 servings.

Mozzarella Baked Omelet

8 eggs
1 C. milk
½ tsp. seasoned salt
3 oz. cooked diced ham

½ C. shredded Cheddar cheese
½ C. shredded mozzarella cheese
1 T. dried minced onion

Preheat the oven to 350°. In a medium bowl, beat together the eggs and milk. Add seasoned salt, diced ham, shredded Cheddar cheese, shredded mozzarella cheese and dried minced onion. Pour mixture into a greased 8″ square baking dish. Bake in the oven, uncovered, for 40 to 45 minutes. Let cool before serving. Makes 4 to 6 servings.

Three-Cheese Breakfast Bake

½ (1 lb.) loaf French bread, cut into 1" cubes
3 T. butter, melted
1 C. shredded Swiss cheese
1 C. shredded Monterey Jack cheese
2 C. diced cooked ham
8 eggs, beaten
1½ C. milk
1 tsp. Dijon mustard
Salt and pepper to taste
¾ C. sour cream
⅓ C. grated Parmesan cheese

Arrange bread cubes in the bottom of a greased 2-quart baking dish and drizzle melted butter over top. Sprinkle with shredded Swiss cheese, shredded Monterey Jack cheese and diced ham. In a medium bowl, blend eggs, milk and Dijon mustard. Season with salt and pepper. Pour mixture into the baking dish, cover and chill in the refrigerator for 8 hours. Preheat the oven to 325°. Remove the dish from the refrigerator and uncover. Bake in the oven for 1 hour or until eggs are set. In a small bowl, blend sour cream and Parmesan cheese and set aside. Remove baking dish from the oven and spread the sour cream mixture over top. Return to the oven and bake 10 minutes more or until surface is lightly browned. Allow to cool 15 minutes before serving. Makes 10 servings.

Sausage, Egg and Cheese Casserole

1 lb. ground pork sausage
1 (8 oz.) tube refrigerated crescent rolls
8 eggs, beaten
2 C. shredded mozzarella cheese
2 C. shredded Cheddar cheese
1 tsp. dried oregano

Preheat the oven to 325°. In a medium skillet over medium-high heat, cook sausage until browned. Drain grease from skillet; crumble sausage and set aside. Unroll the crescent rolls and press into the bottom of a greased 9 x 13" baking dish and sprinkle crumbled sausage over top. In a large bowl, mix eggs, shredded mozzarella cheese and shredded Cheddar cheese. Season the mixture with dried oregano and pour over the sausage and crescent rolls. Bake in the oven for 25 to 30 minutes or until the eggs are set. Makes 10 to 12 servings.

Colby-Jack Breakfast Pizza

1 lb. ground pork sausage
1 (8 oz.) tube refrigerated crescent rolls
1 (10 oz.) can diced tomatoes with green chile peppers, drained
1 (6 oz.) can sliced mushrooms, drained
2½ C. shredded Colby-Jack cheese, divided
6 eggs
1 tsp. Worcestershire sauce
Salt and pepper to taste

Preheat the oven to 350°. In a medium skillet over medium-high heat, cook sausage until browned. Drain grease from skillet; crumble sausage and set aside. Unroll the crescent rolls and press into the bottom of a greased 9 x 13″ baking dish. Cover rolls with sausage, tomatoes, sliced mushrooms and 2 cups shredded Colby-Jack cheese. Bake in the oven for 8 to 10 minutes or until crust is golden brown. In a large bowl, beat together eggs, Worcestershire sauce, salt and pepper. Remove baking dish from oven and pour egg mixture over crust. Bake for 7 to 9 minutes more or until eggs are set. Remove from oven and sprinkle with remaining shredded cheese before serving. Makes 6 servings.

Vanilla Cheese Pancakes

¾ C. flour
⅓ C. sugar
5 eggs
1 T. vanilla extract

Pinch of salt
1 (16 oz.) container cottage cheese
1 tsp. baking powder
1 to 2 T. vegetable oil

In a large bowl, mix together flour, sugar, eggs, vanilla, salt, cottage cheese and baking powder. In a large skillet over medium heat, warm oil. Drop batter by the tablespoonful onto the skillet and fry pancakes until golden brown on both sides. Drain pancakes on paper towels before serving. Makes 4 to 6 servings.

French Toast Surprise

6 (2" thick) slices French bread
¼ C. ricotta cheese
¼ C. cottage cheese, whipped
2 T. cream cheese, softened

2 tsp. sugar
2 tsp. vanilla extract
3 C. egg substitute
¼ C. evaporated milk

Slice an opening into the crust of each piece of French bread to create a pocket and open carefully. In a large bowl, combine the ricotta cheese, whipped cottage cheese and cream cheese. Add the sugar and vanilla and beat until smooth. Gently stuff the mixture into the pocket of each slice of French bread. In a medium bowl, beat together the egg substitute and milk. Dip the slices of bread in the egg mixture. Coat a medium skillet in non-stick cooking spray. Place the skillet over medium-high heat and cook the toast for 3 to 4 minutes on each side or until golden brown. Serve French toast warm. Makes 6 servings.

Crabby Cheddar Casserole

2 eggs, beaten
2 C. milk
2 C. seasoned croutons
1 (8 oz.) pkg. shredded Cheddar cheese
1 T. dried minced onion
1 T. dried parsley
1 lb. fresh crabmeat
Salt and pepper to taste
¼ C. grated Parmesan cheese

Preheat the oven to 325°. In a large bowl, mix eggs, milk, seasoned croutons, shredded Cheddar cheese, minced onion and dried parsley. Stir in the fresh crabmeat and season with salt and pepper. Spoon the mixture into a greased 2-quart baking dish and sprinkle grated Parmesan cheese over top. Bake in the oven for 1 hour or until eggs are set. Serve casserole warm. Makes 8 servings.

Horseradish and Cheese Omelet

2 eggs
1 tsp. salt-free herb seasoning blend
1½ tsp. prepared horseradish

½ C. shredded Cheddar cheese
¼ C. grated Parmesan cheese

In a medium bowl, whisk together the eggs and herb seasoning blend. Warm a lightly greased skillet over medium-high heat. Pour the egg mixture into skillet and rotate to coat evenly. Cook egg mixture until almost done, then flip. Spread horseradish over top and sprinkle with shredded Cheddar cheese and grated Parmesan cheese. Continue to cook until the bottom is no longer raw. Fold in half and transfer to a plate to serve. Makes 1 serving.

Ham and Swiss Pie Casserole

1 lb. bacon
1½ C. diced cooked ham
2 C. shredded Swiss cheese
1 C. shredded Cheddar cheese
1 onion, chopped

4 eggs, beaten
1 C. biscuit baking mix
½ tsp. salt
¼ tsp. pepper

Preheat the oven to 400°. In a medium skillet over medium-high heat, cook bacon until crisp and browned. Drain grease from skillet; crumble bacon and set aside. In a greased 9 x 13" baking dish, mix the bacon, ham, Swiss cheese, Cheddar cheese and onion. In a medium bowl, mix the eggs, biscuit baking mix, salt and pepper. Pour biscuit mixture over the ingredients in the baking dish. Bake in the oven for 25 minutes or until top is golden brown and eggs are set. Serve casserole warm. Makes 8 servings.

American Egg Sandwich

1 egg
1 T. milk
Salt and pepper to taste

2 slices white bread, toasted
1 slice American cheese

In a microwave-safe bowl, whisk together the egg and milk. Season with salt and pepper. Cook in the microwave on full power for 1 to 2 minutes or until cooked throughout. Using a spoon, remove the cooked egg from the bowl and set it on one piece of toast. Top egg with the American cheese slice and the remaining piece of toast. Cook in the microwave for 15 seconds until cheese is melted. Serve sandwich immediately. Makes 1 serving.

Feta Cheese Eggs

1 T. butter
¼ C. chopped onion
4 eggs, beaten
¼ C. chopped tomatoes
2 T. crumbled feta cheese
Salt and pepper to taste

In a medium skillet over medium-high heat, melt butter. Add onions and cook until tender. Pour in eggs and cook, stirring occasionally, to scramble. When eggs appear almost done, stir in chopped tomatoes and feta cheese; season with salt and pepper. Cook until cheese is melted and spoon onto a plate to serve immediately. Makes 1 to 2 servings.

Cheese and Egg Puffs

1 lb. bacon
10 eggs, beaten
1 (16 oz.) container cottage cheese
1 (16 oz.) pkg. shredded Monterey Jack cheese
1 (7 oz.) can diced green chile peppers, drained

½ C. flour
½ C. butter, melted
1 tsp. baking powder
½ tsp. salt

In a medium skillet over medium-high heat, cook bacon until crisp and browned. Drain grease from skillet, crumble bacon and set aside. In a large bowl, combine eggs, cottage cheese, shredded Monterey Jack cheese, diced chile peppers and crumbled bacon. Cover and chill in the refrigerator overnight. Preheat the oven to 350°. Remove cheese mixture from refrigerator and stir in flour, melted butter, baking powder and salt. Spoon batter into 24 greased muffin cups. Bake in the oven for 25 to 30 minutes or until puffs are slightly golden on top. Remove from muffin cups and serve immediately. Makes 24 servings.

Salads, Soups and Sides

Cheesy Italian Taco Salad

1 lb. ground beef
3 C. crushed tortilla chips
2 C. shredded mozzarella cheese
2 C. shredded Cheddar cheese
1 (10 oz.) pkg. mixed salad greens
1 (8 oz.) bottle zesty Italian dressing

In a medium skillet over medium heat, cook the ground beef until browned. Drain grease from skillet. In a large bowl, combine the ground beef, tortilla chips, shredded mozzarella cheese, shredded Cheddar cheese and salad greens. Toss with zesty Italian dressing until evenly coated and serve. Makes 6 servings.

Three-Cheese Lettuce Salad

1 large head lettuce, rinsed, dried and torn into bite-size pieces
1 C. cubed Swiss cheese
1 C. crumbled feta cheese
1 C. shredded Parmesan cheese
1 C. toasted pecan pieces*
½ C. olive oil
½ C. white balsamic vinegar
1 T. Italian seasoning
1 to 2 tsp. pepper, add more to taste

In a large bowl combine lettuce, cubed Swiss cheese, crumbled feta cheese, shredded Parmesan cheese and toasted pecans. In a small bowl, whisk together olive oil, white balsamic vinegar, Italian seasoning and pepper. Add dressing to salad and toss well before serving. Makes 6 servings.

*To toast, place pecan pieces in a single layer on a baking sheet. Bake at 350° for approximately 10 minutes or until pecan pieces are golden brown.

Pasta, Tomato and Mozzarella Salad

1 (12 oz.) pkg. penne pasta
¼ C. olive oil
1 bunch green onions, chopped
1 clove garlic, minced
1 C. quartered cherry tomatoes

Salt and pepper to taste
5 oz. mozzarella cheese, diced
½ C. grated Parmesan cheese
4 oz. fresh basil
12 large black olives, halved

Bring a pot of lightly salted water to a boil. Add penne pasta and cook 8 to 10 minutes or until tender. Drain water from pot and set aside. In a small saucepan over medium-high heat, warm olive oil. Add chopped green onions and cook for 2 to 3 minutes. Stir in minced garlic and cook for 2 minutes more. Add penne pasta, quartered cherry tomatoes, salt and pepper. Reduce heat to low and cook until heated throughout. Stir in diced mozzarella and shredded Parmesan cheese. Coarsely tear basil leaves in halves or thirds. Add torn basil leaves and halved olives to mixture. Serve immediately. Makes 6 servings.

Cottage Cheese and Cucumber Salad

1 (16 oz.) container cottage cheese, drained
4 Roma tomatoes, chopped
4 green onions, chopped
2 medium cucumbers, peeled and diced
Salt and pepper to taste

In a medium bowl, combine the cottage cheese, chopped Roma tomatoes, chopped green onions and diced cucumbers. Season with salt and pepper to taste. Chill in the refrigerator until ready to serve. Makes 4 servings.

Gorgonzola Salad

8 oz. Gorgonzola cheese, crumbled
½ tsp. dried oregano
1 clove garlic, crushed
½ tsp. dried tarragon
½ tsp. dried basil
⅓ C. olive oil
1 C. milk
1 T. red wine vinegar
2 heads Boston lettuce, cored and shredded
1 avocado, diced
¼ C. chopped walnuts

In a blender or food processor, blend together crumbled Gorgonzola cheese, dried oregano, crushed garlic, dried tarragon, dried basil, olive oil, milk and red wine vinegar until smooth. In a large bowl, toss the Gorgonzola dressing with shredded lettuce, diced avocado and walnuts. Chill in the refrigerator until ready to serve. Makes 6 servings.

Easy Cheesy Pea Salad

1 (15 oz.) can peas, drained
4 oz. Cheddar cheese, cubed
2 T. minced sweet onion

1 T. sugar
¼ C. mayonnaise

In a medium bowl, mix together peas, cubed Cheddar cheese and minced sweet onion. Stir in the sugar and mayonnaise. Chill in the refrigerator for 1 hour before serving. Makes 8 servings.

Red, White and Blue Cheese Slaw

6 C. green cabbage, coarsely shredded
½ C. bacon bits
¾ C. crumbled blue cheese, divided

1 C. cole slaw dressing
Cherry tomatoes, optional

In a large bowl, combine shredded green cabbage, bacon bits and ½ cup blue cheese. Add cole slaw dressing and toss gently to coat. Chill in the refrigerator for 1 hour. Before serving, sprinkle the remaining ¼ cup crumbled blue cheese over top. Garnish with cherry tomatoes, if desired. Makes 8 servings.

Parmesan Garlic Broccoli

4 cloves garlic, peeled
1½ tsp. salt
⅓ C. olive oil
¼ C. red wine vinegar
1 T. Dijon mustard
1 bunch broccoli, cut into florets
½ C. grated Parmesan cheese

Place peeled garlic cloves on a cutting board and sprinkle with salt. Using a pestle or flat side of a knife, mash together garlic and salt until a paste forms. Transfer to a medium bowl and stir in olive oil, red wine vinegar and mustard. Add broccoli and stir to coat. Chill in the refrigerator for 3 hours, stirring occasionally. Sprinkle grated Parmesan cheese over top of the salad before serving. Makes 8 servings.

Smoked Gouda and Salad Greens

⅓ C. balsamic vinegar
⅓ C. olive oil
¼ C. soy sauce
2 cloves garlic, pressed
2 T. chopped fresh basil

8 oz. smoked Gouda cheese, cubed
2 tomatoes, cut into wedges
1 (10 oz.) pkg. mixed salad greens
¼ tsp. pepper

In a medium bowl, stir together the balsamic vinegar, olive oil, soy sauce, pressed garlic and chopped fresh basil. Add cubed Gouda cheese and tomatoes; toss to coat. Cover and chill in the refrigerator for 30 minutes. To serve, divide salad greens and place on individual serving plates. Top with the Gouda cheese dressing and season with pepper. Makes 6 servings.

Swiss Mushroom Salad

½ C. olive oil
⅓ C. red wine vinegar
1 T. Dijon mustard
1 lb. fresh white mushrooms

1 C. sliced celery
¼ C. chopped fresh parsley
¼ C. diced Swiss cheese
½ C. chopped green onions

In a large bowl, whisk together the olive oil, red wine vinegar and Dijon mustard. Add mushrooms, sliced celery, chopped fresh parsley, diced Swiss cheese and chopped green onions; toss to coat. Chill in the refrigerator for 2 hours before serving. Makes 6 servings.

Cheesy Potato Soup

6 T. unsalted butter
1½ C. chopped onions
1½ C. chopped celery
8 potatoes, peeled and cubed
15 slices American cheese,
  torn into pieces

4 T. flour
2⅓ C. milk
2 T. chopped fresh parsley

In a large pot over medium heat, melt butter. Add chopped onions and celery; cook 5 to 10 minutes or until tender. Stir in 4 cups of water and cubed potatoes. Bring to a boil and let simmer until the potatoes are tender. Add pieces of American cheese and stir until melted. In a small bowl, combine the flour and milk; stir until the flour is dissolved. Pour mixture into the soup slowly and stir continuously for 5 minutes or until soup has thickened. To serve, garnish with parsley. Makes 8 servings.

Vegetable Cheese Soup

2 C. chopped carrots
2 C. chopped celery
2 C. chopped onion
2 C. chicken broth

1 C. margarine, softened
½ C. plus 2 T. cornstarch
1 gal. milk
4 lb. processed cheese, cubed

In a large pot over medium-high heat, cook the chopped carrots, chopped celery, chopped onion and chicken broth for 15 minutes or until vegetables are tender. In a small bowl, combine the margarine and cornstarch; set aside. In a small saucepan over medium heat, warm the milk, but do not bring to a boil. Slowly add the cornstarch and margarine mixture to the milk; stir until smooth. Add milk mixture to the vegetables and continue to cook over medium heat. Slowly add the cubed cheese to the soup, stirring constantly until cheese is melted. Serve the soup warm. Makes 20 servings.

Broccoli Cheese Soup

2 C. chicken broth
2½ C. chopped fresh broccoli
¼ C. chopped onion
1 C. milk

2 T. flour
1 C. shredded Cheddar cheese
½ tsp. dried oregano
Salt and pepper to taste

In a large pot over medium-high heat, bring chicken broth to a boil. Add broccoli and onion. Cook for 5 minutes or until broccoli is tender. In a medium bowl, slowly add milk to flour and mix until well blended. Stir flour mixture into broth mixture. Cook, stirring constantly, until soup is thick and bubbly. Add shredded Cheddar cheese; stir until melted. Season with salt and pepper before serving. Makes 5 servings.

Gruyère French Onion Soup

¼ C. butter
2 onions, thinly sliced
2 T. flour
2 (10.5 oz.) cans beef broth

6 slices French bread, toasted*
½ C. grated Parmesan cheese
½ C. shredded Gruyère cheese**

Preheat the oven to 425°. In a medium saucepan over medium heat, warm the butter. Add the sliced onions and cook until tender. Stir in flour. Gradually add beef broth and 2½ cups of water. Bring the mixture to a boil and let simmer for 20 minutes. Place 1 piece of toasted bread in each of 6 individual, oven-safe soup bowls. Pour soup mixture over bread and sprinkle with grated Parmesan and shredded Gruyère cheese. Bake in the oven for 10 minutes. Remove from oven and serve warm. Makes 6 servings.

*To toast, place French bread slices in a single layer on a baking sheet. Bake at 350° for approximately 5 minutes or until crisp and golden brown.

**Gruyère cheese is a hard yellow Swiss cheese made from cow's milk. It is named after a district in Switzerland. It is sweet but slightly salty, with a flavor that varies widely with age and is known as a fine cheese for baking.

Chunky Cheese Soup

2 C. peeled and diced potatoes
½ C. diced carrots
½ C. chopped celery
¼ C. chopped onions
1½ tsp. salt
¼ tsp. pepper

1 C. cooked cubed ham
¼ C. butter
¼ C. flour
2 C. milk
2 C. shredded Cheddar cheese

In a large saucepan over medium-high heat, combine 2 cups of water, diced potatoes, diced carrots, chopped celery, chopped onions, salt and pepper; bring to a boil. Reduce heat and simmer 30 minutes or until vegetables are tender. Add cubed ham to the vegetable mixture. In a medium saucepan over medium heat, melt the butter. Stir in the flour until smooth. Pour in the milk slowly, stirring constantly, and bring to a boil. Cook and stir for 2 minutes or until mixture has thickened. Add shredded Cheddar cheese and stir until melted. Add the melted cheese mixture to the vegetable mixture and stir until combined. Serve soup immediately. Makes 8 servings.

Leek, Potato and Mushroom Soup

- 2 T. butter, divided
- 1 T. olive oil
- 2 leeks, finely chopped (white part only)
- 1 clove garlic, minced
- 4 medium red potatoes, chopped
- 1½ tsp. ground mustard
- 2 T. flour
- Salt and pepper to taste
- Celery salt to taste
- 3 C. chicken broth
- ½ C. shredded Cheddar cheese
- 2 T. grated Parmesan cheese
- 1 C. milk
- 3 oz. Portobello mushrooms, chopped
- Croutons, optional

In a large pot over medium-low heat, warm 1 tablespoon of butter and olive oil. Add chopped leek, minced garlic and chopped red potatoes. Cook, stirring constantly, until vegetables are tender. In a medium bowl, combine ground mustard, flour, salt, pepper and celery salt. Whisk in ½ cup of water and chicken broth. Add to potato mixture and bring to a boil. Reduce heat and let simmer for 1 hour. Gently mash potatoes by hand so they remain lumpy. Stir in shredded Cheddar cheese and grated Parmesan cheese until melted. Add milk to the soup but do not bring to a boil. In a medium skillet over medium-low heat, warm remaining 1 tablespoon of butter. Add chopped Portobello mushrooms and cook until tender. Stir Portobello mushrooms into soup. To serve, garnish with croutons if desired. Makes 6 servings.

Cauliflower Cheese Soup

1 C. chopped cauliflower
1 C. cubed potatoes
½ C. finely chopped celery
½ C. diced carrots
¼ C. chopped onion

¼ C. butter
¼ C. flour
3 C. milk
Salt and pepper to taste
4 oz. shredded Cheddar cheese

In a large saucepan over medium-high heat, combine ¾ cup water, chopped cauliflower, cubed potatoes, finely chopped celery, diced carrots and chopped onion. Boil for 5 to 10 minutes or until vegetables are tender; set aside, but do not drain. In a large saucepan over medium heat, melt butter. Stir in flour and cook for 2 minutes. Remove flour mixture from heat and slowly stir in milk. Return to heat and cook until thickened. Stir in vegetables and water; season with salt and pepper. Add shredded Cheddar cheese and stir until melted. Serve immediately. Makes 4 servings.

Outback Onion Soup

8 beef bouillon cubes, crumbled
2 large onions, quartered and sliced
1 tsp. salt
1 tsp. pepper
¾ C. flour
1 C. heavy cream
1½ C. shredded Colby-Jack cheese
Croutons, if desired

In a large pot over medium heat, bring 2 quarts of water to a boil. Stir in beef bouillon cubes and let boil for 10 minutes or until dissolved. Place onions in boiling water, reduce heat and simmer for 30 minutes. Stir in salt and pepper; simmer 30 minutes more. In a small bowl, mix the flour and ½ cup cold water to make a paste. Gently whisk the flour mixture into the simmering soup. Be careful not to break the onions. Simmer 30 minutes more. Stir in heavy cream and shredded Colby-Jack cheese; cook until cheese is melted and mixture is heated throughout. Serve hot and garnish with croutons if desired. Makes 4 servings.

Wild Rice Soup

1 lb. ground Italian sausage
1 small onion, diced
1 C. uncooked wild rice
1 (10.75 oz.) can cream of potato soup
1 (10.75 oz.) can cream of chicken soup
1 C. milk
1 C. evaporated milk
1 lb. processed cheese, cubed

In a medium skillet over medium-high heat, cook the Italian sausage and onions until sausage is browned and onion is tender. Drain grease from skillet and set aside. In a small saucepan over medium-high heat, bring 2 cups of water to a boil. Add rice and simmer until water has evaporated. In a large stockpot over low heat, combine the cooked sausage and onions, cooked rice, cream of potato soup, cream of chicken soup, milk and evaporated milk; cook until heated throughout. Add the processed cheese and stir occasionally until cheese is melted. Serve soup immediately. Makes 12 servings.

Cheddar Crabmeat Soup

2 T. margarine
2 T. flour
¼ tsp. salt
Pinch of pepper
4 C. milk

8 oz. shredded Cheddar cheese
1 dash hot pepper sauce
1 (6 oz.) can crab meat, drained
1 T. chopped green onions

In a large saucepan over medium heat, melt the margarine. Add the flour and stir well until a paste forms. Season with salt and pepper. Slowly add the milk and stir constantly until mixture thickens. Do not let the mixture scorch. Add the shredded Cheddar cheese and stir until all the cheese melts and mixture is smooth. Stir in the hot pepper sauce and crab meat; cook until heated throughout. To serve, ladle soup into individual bowls and sprinkle green onions over top. Makes 4 servings.

Three-Cheese Mashed Potatoes

1 (3 oz.) can bacon bits, divided
4 C. prepared mashed potatoes
2 C. shredded Cheddar cheese
4 slices American cheese, torn into pieces
¾ C. grated Parmesan cheese
1 medium onion, minced
Salt and pepper to taste
Pinch of garlic powder
¼ C. butter, melted
¼ C. grated Parmesan cheese
1 C. dry bread crumbs
Pinch of onion powder

Preheat the oven to 350°. Measure 1 tablespoon of bacon bits and set aside. In a 2-quart baking dish, stir together prepared mashed potatoes, shredded Cheddar cheese, pieces of American cheese, grated Parmesan cheese, remaining bacon bits, minced onion, salt, pepper and garlic powder until cheeses begin to melt. In a small bowl, combine melted butter, grated Parmesan cheese, reserved 1 tablespoon of bacon bits, dry bread crumbs and onion powder. Sprinkle the mixture over the potatoes. Bake in the oven for 30 minutes or until the topping has browned. To serve, spoon potatoes onto individual dinner plates. Makes 6 servings.

Layered Cheesy Macaroni

1 (8 oz.) can tomato sauce
1 (16 oz.) can tomatoes, in juice
1 small onion, minced
½ tsp. salt
¼ tsp. pepper
1¼ tsp. dried oregano
1 (8 oz.) pkg. shell pasta
1 (16 oz.) container cottage cheese
1 (8 oz.) pkg. shredded mozzarella cheese
½ C. grated Parmesan cheese

Preheat the oven to 375°. In a medium saucepan over medium heat, combine the tomato sauce, canned tomatoes, minced onion, salt, pepper and oregano; stirring occasionally. Cover and simmer for 20 minutes. Bring a large pot of lightly salted water to a boil. Add shell pasta and cook for 8 to 10 minutes or until al dente. Drain water from pot and set aside. Place ⅓ of the cooked shell pasta in the bottom of a greased 3-quart baking dish. Spread a layer of cottage cheese over the pasta. Pour ⅓ of the tomato sauce over the cottage cheese. Place another ⅓ of the shell pasta over the sauce. Sprinkle the mozzarella cheese over top and pour another ⅓ of the sauce over the cheese. Add the remaining ⅓ of shell pasta and sprinkle the grated Parmesan over the top. Pour the last ⅓ of the sauce over the Parmesan cheese and bake in oven for 45 minutes. Let cool slightly before serving. Makes 8 servings.

Parmesan Baked Zucchini

1 large zucchini, cut lengthwise, then in half
1 (8 oz.) pkg. cream cheese, softened
1 C. sour cream
¼ C. grated Parmesan cheese
1 T. minced garlic
Paprika to taste

Preheat the oven to 350°. Bring a large pot of water to a boil. Add zucchini and cook for 15 minutes or until tender but still firm. Drain water from pot. Let zucchini cool and scoop out seeds. In a medium bowl, combine cream cheese, sour cream, grated Parmesan cheese and minced garlic. Spoon Parmesan cheese mixture into zucchini halves and sprinkle with paprika. Bake in the oven for 10 to 15 minutes or until heated throughout. Serve immediately. Makes 4 servings.

Chèvre Green Bean Casserole

- 1 (16 oz.) pkg. frozen French-style green beans
- ½ C. cottage cheese
- ½ C. chèvre cheese* with garlic and herbs
- ½ C. slivered almonds, toasted**
- ¼ C. grated Parmesan cheese
- Pepper to taste

Preheat the oven to 375°. In a medium pot over medium-high heat, bring ⅔ cup of water to a boil. Add French-style green beans and return water to a boil. Cook for 10 to 12 minutes or until tender. Drain water from pot and set aside. In a blender, mix cottage cheese and chèvre cheese. In a 2-quart baking dish, combine green beans, cheese mixture and almonds. Sprinkle grated Parmesan cheese over top and season with pepper. Bake in the oven for 20 minutes. Turn oven off and turn the broiler on low. Brown the casserole under the broiler for 3 minutes. Remove from oven and serve immediately. Makes 6 servings.

*Chèvre cheese is cheese made from goat's milk. Chèvre is the French word for goat.

**To toast, place slivered almonds in a single layer on a baking sheet. Bake at 350° for approximately 10 minutes or until almonds are golden brown.

Warm Cheddar Corn

1 C. butter
2 (8 oz.) pkgs. cream cheese
½ C. milk
4 (15 oz.) cans whole kernel corn, drained
1 (12 oz.) jar jalapeno peppers, drained and diced
2 C. shredded Cheddar cheese

Preheat the oven to 375°. In a medium saucepan over medium heat, combine butter, cream cheese and milk. Stir until smooth. In a 9 x 13" baking dish, mix whole kernel corn and diced jalapenos. Pour milk mixture over corn and diced jalepenos. Sprinkle shredded Cheddar cheese over top and bake in the oven for 35 minutes. Remove from oven and serve immediately. Makes 12 servings.

Cheese Stuffed Potatoes

2 medium potatoes
1 small onion, minced
½ C. cottage cheese
¼ C. buttermilk

3 T. grated Parmesan cheese
Salt and pepper to taste
2 T. sliced green onions

Preheat the oven to 400°. Using a fork, pierce holes in the potatoes. Bake potatoes in the oven for 1 hour or until tender. Cut a thin slice off the top of each potato and discard. Scoop out the inside of the potato, set the shell aside and mash the insides in a small bowl. In a large skillet over medium-high heat, cook minced onion in 2 tablespoons of water until tender. Add mashed potatoes, cottage cheese, buttermilk, grated Parmesan cheese, salt and pepper to the onion. Stir and cook until heated throughout. Spoon mixture back into empty potato shells. Sprinkle sliced green onions over top of the potatoes before serving. Makes 2 servings.

Mozzarella Eggplant Au Gratin

½ lb. eggplant, peeled and
  cut into ¼" slices
1 T. olive oil
¾ C. spaghetti sauce, divided

¾ C. shredded mozzarella cheese,
  divided
2 T. shredded Parmesan cheese

Preheat the oven to 400°. Brush both sides of eggplant slices with olive oil. Place eggplant slices on a baking sheet. Bake in the oven for 8 minutes. Turn slices and bake 7 to 8 minutes longer or until lightly browned and tender. Cool eggplant slices on a wire rack. Reduce oven heat to 350°. Place one eggplant slice in each of 2 greased 10-ounce ramekins. Top each eggplant slice with 2 tablespoons of spaghetti sauce, then 2 tablespoons of shredded mozzarella cheese. Repeat layers twice. Sprinkle shredded Parmesan cheese over top of the mozzarella cheese in each dish. Bake in the oven for 20 to 25 minutes or until bubbly and cheese is melted. Makes 2 servings.

Swiss Cheese Green Beans

- 4 C. frozen French-style green beans
- 1 C. canned bean sprouts
- 1 (8 oz.) can sliced water chestnuts, drained
- 2 T. butter
- 2 T. flour
- ¼ tsp. salt
- ⅛ tsp. pepper
- Dash of cayenne pepper
- 1½ C. half-and-half
- ½ tsp. Worcestershire sauce
- ½ C. sliced almonds
- ¼ C. shredded Swiss cheese
- ¼ C. grated Parmesan cheese

Preheat the broiler. In a medium pot over medium-high heat, bring ⅔ cup of water to a boil. Add French-style green beans and return water to a boil. Cook for 10 to 12 minutes or until tender. Add bean sprouts and water chestnuts. Cook until heated throughout. Drain water from pot and set aside. In a medium saucepan, melt butter. Stir in flour, salt, pepper and cayenne pepper until smooth. Slowly add half-and-half. Bring mixture to a boil; cook and stir for 2 minutes or until thickened. Add Worcestershire sauce and green bean mixture; toss to coat. Pour into a greased 2-quart baking dish. In a small bowl, combine sliced almonds, shredded Swiss cheese and grated Parmesan cheese. Sprinkle cheese mixture over green beans. Broil, 4 to 6″ from heat source, for 5 minutes or until almonds are golden brown and cheese is bubbly. Serve immediately. Makes 6 servings.

Zesty Pepper Jack Zucchini

½ C. seasoned bread crumbs, divided
2 lbs. zucchini, thinly sliced
8 oz. Monterey Jack cheese, cubed
8 oz. Pepper Jack cheese, cubed
6 eggs
¾ C. milk
¾ tsp. salt
3 tsp. baking powder
5 T. flour
1 T. butter

Preheat the oven to 325°. Spread half of the bread crumbs in a greased 9 x 13″ baking dish. Place the sliced zucchini in the dish. Sprinkle Monterey Jack and Pepper Jack cheese over sliced zucchini. In a medium bowl, mix together the eggs, milk, salt, baking powder and flour. Spoon mixture over the top of the casserole and dot with butter. Sprinkle remaining bread crumbs over the butter. Bake in the oven for 45 minutes or until the topping is cooked throughout. Serve casserole warm. Makes 8 servings.

Scrumptious Ricotta Stuffed Zucchini

8 zucchini, cut in half lengthwise
2 T. butter, divided
1 small onion, minced
1 clove garlic, minced
1 (10 oz.) pkg. frozen chopped spinach, thawed and drained
2 C. ricotta cheese
2 eggs, beaten
¼ C. grated Parmesan cheese
1 T. chopped parsley
½ tsp. salt
½ tsp. dried basil
½ tsp. dried oregano
Pepper to taste
1 (8 oz.) can tomato sauce

Preheat the oven to 350°. Trim ends of zucchini halves and scoop out insides leaving ½″ of pulp on skins. In a large saucepan with a vegetable steamer, bring water to a boil. Place zucchini halves in steamer and steam for 5 minutes or until tender. Immediately plunge zucchini in a large bowl of ice water and cover. Soak zucchini until completely cooled. Drain water from zucchini and set aside. In a medium saucepan over medium heat, melt 1 tablespoon of butter. Add onion and garlic; cook until tender. Stir in spinach and cook 1 minute more or until spinach is wilted. Transfer spinach mixture to a medium bowl and mix in ricotta cheese, eggs, grated Parmesan cheese, chopped parsley, salt, dried basil, dried oregano and pepper. Stuff zucchini halves with a portion of the mixture and arrange halves in a 9 x 13″ baking dish. In a small saucepan over medium heat, melt the remaining 1 tablespoon of butter. Drizzle the melted butter over the stuffed zucchini. Bake in the oven for 10 minutes or until the stuffing is hot and bubbly. In a small saucepan, heat tomato sauce. Remove zucchini from oven and drizzle tomato sauce over top. Bake for 10 minutes more before serving. Makes 8 servings.

Green Tomatoes and Goat Cheese

4 medium green tomatoes
1 T. balsamic vinegar
2 tsp. minced fresh oregano
1 C. crumbled goat cheese
   (feta or chèvre)

4 tsp. olive oil
Salt and pepper to taste

Preheat the broiler. Cut green tomatoes into ½″ thick slices. Place green tomato slices in a single layer in the bottom of a greased 9 x 13″ baking dish. Some edges may be overlapping. Sprinkle balsamic vinegar and minced fresh oregano over top of the tomatoes. Top with crumbled goat cheese and drizzle with olive oil. Broil, 5 to 8″ from heat, for 7 to 8 minutes or until cheese starts to brown. Season with salt and pepper before serving. Makes 8 servings.

Main Dishes

Cheddar Apple Pork Chops

1 large apple, peeled, cored and cubed
1 T. sugar
2 pork chops
¼ C. shredded Cheddar Cheese

Preheat the grill to medium-high heat and brush the grill grate with oil. In a small saucepan over low heat, combine cubed apples, 2 tablespoons of water and sugar. Cover and cook for 10 to 20 minutes, stirring occasionally, or until apples are pulpy. Cook pork chops on the grill for 5 to 10 minutes on each side or until cooked throughout. While still on the grill, spoon some of the cooked apples onto each pork chop. Sprinkle some shredded Cheddar cheese over the apple mixture and continue heating until cheese is melted and bubbly. Place pork chops on dinner plates and serve immediately. Makes 2 servings.

Blue Cheese Steak

4 New York strip steaks
¼ tsp. salt
1 (6 oz.) pkg. crumbled blue cheese

2 T. butter, softened
1 T. chopped fresh parsley

Preheat the grill to medium-high heat. Season New York strip steaks with salt. Cook on the grill for 6 minutes on each side or until internal temperature reaches 145°. In a small bowl, combine crumbled blue cheese and butter; blend until creamy. Spread blue cheese mixture over steaks and cook for an additional 30 seconds or until topping begins to melt. Sprinkle chopped parsley over top before serving. Makes 4 servings.

Three-Cheese Grilled Cheese

2 tsp. butter
2 slices rye bread
1 slice Cheddar cheese
1 slice Muenster cheese
1 slice provolone cheese

Preheat the broiler to low. Spread 1 teaspoon of butter over one side of each slice of bread. Place each slice of bread, butter side down, on a baking sheet. Place the Cheddar cheese and Muenster cheese on one slice of bread and the provolone cheese on the other slice. Cook under the broiler for 5 to 10 minutes or until cheese is bubbly and slightly brown. Remove from the broiler and press the 2 pieces of bread together, cheese to cheese. Let cool slightly before serving. Makes 1 serving.

Cheesy Baked Ziti

8 oz. ziti pasta
2 C. half-and-half
½ tsp. dried basil
¼ tsp. crushed red pepper flakes
1¼ C. shredded provolone cheese

1¼ C. shredded mozzarella cheese
1¼ C. shredded Swiss cheese
2 T. grated Parmesan cheese
2 egg yolks, beaten
Salt and pepper to taste

Preheat the oven to 375°. Bring a large pot of lightly salted water to a boil. Add ziti pasta and cook 8 to 10 minutes or until al dente. Drain water from pot and set aside. In a large saucepan over medium-high heat, combine half-and-half, dried basil and crushed red pepper flakes; bring to a simmer. Slowly add shredded provolone cheese, shredded mozzarella cheese, shredded Swiss cheese and grated Parmesan cheese one at a time. Cook, stirring constantly, until cheese is melted. Remove saucepan from heat and stir in egg yolks. Season with salt and pepper; stir in pasta. Transfer mixture to a greased 2-quart baking dish. Bake in the oven for 10 minutes or until heated throughout and eggs are cooked. Serve baked ziti hot. Makes 4 servings.

Lasagna Roll-ups

- 1 (16 oz.) box uncooked lasagna noodles
- 1 (16 oz.) pkg. shredded mozzarella cheese
- 1 (15 oz.) container ricotta cheese
- 1 lb. firm tofu, cut up
- 1 (10 oz.) pkg. frozen chopped spinach, thawed, drained and squeezed dry
- 2 C. grated Parmesan cheese, divided
- 1 (28 oz.) jar spaghetti sauce

Preheat the oven to 350°. Bring a pot of lightly salted water to a boil. Add lasagna noodles and cook for 8 to 10 minutes or until al dente. In a large mixing bowl, combine shredded mozzarella cheese, ricotta cheese, tofu, chopped spinach and 1 cup grated Parmesan cheese. Lay 1 cooked lasagna noodle out and spread a layer of the cheese mixture over the noodle. Pour a thin layer of spaghetti sauce over the cheese and roll the noodle up. Place the lasagna roll, seam side down, in a 9 x 13" baking dish. Repeat the process with the remaining lasagna noodles. Sprinkle the remaining 1 cup of grated Parmesan cheese over all the lasagna rolls. Bake in the oven for 30 minutes or until hot and bubbly. To serve, place 1 or 2 lasagna rolls on individual dinner plates. Makes 12 servings.

Cheddar Creole Chicken

- 1 C. crushed cornflakes
- ¾ C. grated Parmesan cheese
- ¼ C. shredded Cheddar cheese
- 1 T. garlic salt
- 1 T. Creole-style seasoning
- ½ tsp. cayenne pepper
- ½ C. butter, melted
- 8 skinless, boneless chicken breast halves

Preheat the oven to 350°. In a large bowl, mix together the crushed cornflakes, grated Parmesan cheese, shredded Cheddar cheese, garlic salt, Creole-style seasoning and cayenne pepper. Pour melted butter into a small shallow bowl. Place each chicken breast in the butter and turn to coat. Roll the chicken breast in the crumb mixture and place in a greased 9 x 13″ baking dish. Bake in the oven for 40 minutes or until chicken is no longer pink and juices run clear. Makes 8 servings.

Mozzarella Chicken Monte Cristo

2 T. honey mustard
8 slices sourdough bread
4 (1 oz.) slices roasted chicken breast
1½ C. shredded mozzarella cheese
½ C. grated Parmesan cheese

2 eggs, beaten
¼ C. milk
¼ tsp. ground nutmeg
1 T. butter

Spread honey mustard over one side of 4 slices of sourdough bread. Top remaining 4 slices of sourdough bread with chicken breast slices. In a medium bowl, combine shredded mozzarella cheese and grated Parmesan cheese. Sprinkle cheese mixture over chicken and close sandwiches with the mustard side down. In a medium shallow bowl, combine the eggs, milk and nutmeg; stir well. In a large skillet over medium heat, melt butter. Dip each sandwich in egg mixture and turn to coat. Let excess egg mixture drip off sandwiches before placing on the skillet. Cook sandwiches in skillet until golden brown on each side and cheese is melted. Makes 4 servings.

Parmesan and Garlic Chicken Roll-ups

4 skinless, boneless chicken breasts
1 C. seasoned dry bread crumbs
½ C. grated Parmesan cheese

¼ C. butter, melted
1 (7 oz.) pkg. garlic cheese spread

Preheat the oven to 350°. Pound each chicken breast until flattened. In a medium shallow bowl, mix together seasoned dry bread crumbs and grated Parmesan cheese. Pour the melted butter into a small shallow bowl. Place the chicken breasts in the melted butter; do not turn to coat. Dip the same side of the chicken breast into the crumb and cheese mixture. On the side not coated in breading, place a dollop of garlic cheese spread at one end of each chicken breast. Roll up each chicken breast and secure with toothpicks. Place the chicken roll-ups in a lightly greased 9 x 13" baking dish and drizzle any remaining butter over the chicken. Bake in the oven for 35 to 40 minutes or until cooked throughout and juices run clear. Makes 4 servings.

Blue Fettuccini Alfredo

1 (16 oz.) pkg. fettuccini
1 T. olive oil
1 clove garlic, sliced
4 oz. crumbled blue cheese
¼ C. grated Parmesan cheese
2 C. heavy cream
1 T. Italian seasoning
Salt and pepper to taste

Bring a large pot of lightly salted water to a boil. Add fettuccini and cook for 8 to 10 minutes or until al dente. Drain water from pot and set pasta aside. In a small skillet over medium heat, warm olive oil. Sauté sliced garlic in olive oil until golden. Remove garlic from skillet and reserve oil. In a medium saucepan over medium-low heat, combine crumbled blue cheese, grated Parmesan cheese and heavy cream; stir until cheese is melted. Stir in the reserved olive oil. Sprinkle with Italian seasoning, salt and pepper. In a large serving bowl, toss together sauce and cooked fettuccini. Let stand for 5 minutes before serving. Makes 8 servings.

Smoked Mozzarella Sandwich

2 T. basil pesto sauce
2 slices sourdough bread, toasted
1 T. mayonnaise
1 T. grated Parmesan cheese
1 slice provolone cheese

¼ C. shredded smoked mozzarella cheese
1 lettuce leaf
2 slices tomato

Spread a thin layer of basil pesto sauce over one side of one of the sourdough bread slices. Spread a thin layer of mayonnaise over one side of the remaining piece of bread. Sprinkle grated Parmesan cheese over the pesto and mayonnaise. Layer the provolone cheese and mozzarella cheese on top of one bread slice. Top with lettuce leaf, tomato slices and the other slice of bread. Makes 1 serving.

Cheesy Chicken Pizza

2 skinless boneless chicken breast halves
1 (10 oz.) tube refrigerated pizza crust
½ C. ranch salad dressing
1 C. shredded mozzarella cheese
1 C. chopped tomatoes
¼ C. chopped green onions
1 C. shredded Cheddar cheese

Preheat the oven to 425°. In a large skillet over medium-high heat, cook the chicken breast halves until no longer pink and juices run clear. Let chicken cool, then shred into small pieces. Unroll the pizza crust dough and press into a greased pizza pan or baking sheet. Bake crust in the oven for 7 minutes or until it begins to turn golden brown. Remove crust from oven. Spread ranch dressing over partially baked crust. Sprinkle shredded mozzarella cheese over the crust. Top with chopped tomatoes, chopped green onion, shredded chicken and sprinkle with shredded Cheddar cheese. Return to the oven for 20 to 25 minutes or until cheese is melted and bubbly. Cut into wedges before serving. Makes 8 servings.

Pasta Cheese Pizza

1 lb. dry vermicelli
1 C. milk
2 eggs, beaten
1 T. garlic salt
1 T. dried parsley
Pepper to taste

2 C. shredded mozzarella cheese, divided
½ C. grated Parmesan cheese
3½ C. spaghetti sauce
1 (8 oz.) pkg. sliced pepperoni

Preheat the oven to 400°. Bring a large pot of lightly salted water to a boil. Break vermicelli into 2″ pieces and cook in water for 8 to 10 minutes or until al dente. Drain water from pot. Spread pasta in a greased 9 x 13″ baking dish. In a medium bowl, combine milk, eggs, garlic salt, dried parsley, pepper and 1 cup of the shredded mozzarella cheese. Pour the mixture over the pasta and sprinkle with the grated Parmesan cheese. Bake in the oven for 15 minutes. Reduce oven heat to 350°. Remove dish from oven and pour spaghetti sauce over pasta; top with sliced pepperoni and remaining 1 cup of shredded mozzarella cheese. Return to oven and cook 10 minutes more or until cheese is completely melted. Makes 8 servings.

Easy Cheesy Lasagna

1 (16 oz.) pkg. uncooked
    lasagna noodles
1 (26 oz.) jar spaghetti sauce
1 (16 oz.) container cottage cheese

1 (8 oz.) pkg. shredded
    mozzarella cheese
1 (8 oz.) pkg. shredded Cheddar cheese
1 C. grated Parmesan cheese

Preheat the oven to 375°. Bring a large pot of lightly salted water to a boil. Add lasagna noodles and cook for 8 to 10 minutes or until al dente. Drain water from pot. Using a blender or an electric mixer, blend together spaghetti sauce and cottage cheese until smooth. Spoon some of the spaghetti sauce mixture into the bottom of a 9 x 13˝ baking dish. Place a layer of cooked noodles over the sauce and sprinkle a portion of the shredded mozzarella cheese, the shredded Cheddar cheese and the grated Parmesan cheese over the noodles. Repeat layers of sauce, noodles and cheese. Finish with a layer of shredded cheese. Bake in the oven for 30 to 45 minutes or until cheese is bubbly and golden. Cut into squares to serve. Makes 8 servings.

Herbed Goat Cheese Salmon

4 salmon fillets
½ C. herbed goat cheese

¼ C. Dijon mustard and mayonnaise blend
Salt and pepper to taste

Preheat the oven to 350°. Arrange the salmon fillets in a greased 9 x 13" baking dish. Make several small incisions in each salmon fillet and stuff equal amounts of the herbed goat cheese into each incision. Spread Dijon mustard and mayonnaise blend over each fillet. Season with salt and pepper. Bake salmon in the oven for 15 minutes or until salmon can be flaked with a fork. Makes 4 servings.

Cheese Stuffed Lobster Tails

2 C. crushed round butter crackers
½ C. chopped cooked shrimp
½ C. butter, melted
4 (6 oz.) raw lobster tails, shelled

1 (10.75 oz.) can cream of shrimp soup
1 C. milk
8 oz. processed cheese, cubed

Preheat the oven to 325°. In a medium bowl, combine the crushed round butter crackers and chopped cooked shrimp. Stir in the melted butter and stir to form a stuffing. Spread stuffing over lobster tail meat and roll meat from one end of the tail to the other. Secure the lobster tails with toothpicks and place in a greased 8″ baking dish. In a medium saucepan over medium heat, combine the cream of shrimp soup, milk and processed cheese cubes. Cook and stir until cheese has melted. Pour mixture over the lobster tails. Top tails with leftover stuffing mixture. Bake in the oven for 25 minutes or until sauce is hot and lobster meat is opaque. Makes 4 servings.

Cheddar Chicken Crescent Rolls

2 (10.75 oz.) cans cream of chicken soup
2½ C. milk
1 C. shredded Cheddar cheese, divided
2 (8 oz.) tubes refrigerated crescent roll dough
2 to 3 C. cooked shredded chicken

Preheat the oven to 350°. In a large saucepan over low heat, combine cream of chicken soup, milk and ½ cup of the shredded Cheddar cheese. Separate crescent rolls into triangles. Place some shredded chicken onto the large end of each crescent roll and top with some of the remaining shredded Cheddar cheese. Roll up the dough and place in a 9 x 13″ baking dish. Pour half the soup mixture directly into the baking dish, but not on top of the rolls. Bake in the oven for 10 to 15 minutes or until rolls rise slightly and are lightly browned. Remove from oven and pour remaining half of the soup mixture into the dish and place any leftover chicken on top. Sprinkle with any remaining shredded Cheddar cheese. Return to oven until rolls are browned and cheese has melted. Makes 8 servings.

Feta Stuffed Chicken Breasts

½ C. olive oil
2 tsp. lemon juice
4 cloves crushed garlic
1 T. dried oregano

Salt and pepper to taste
4 skinless, boneless chicken breasts
4 slices feta cheese
4 slices bacon, fried and drained

Preheat the oven to 350°. In a small bowl combine the olive oil, lemon juice, crushed garlic, dried oregano, salt and pepper; mix together. Slice an opening, like a mouth, into the thick end of each chicken breast. Stuff each chicken breast with 1 slice feta cheese and 1 slice bacon. Place chicken in a 9 x 13" baking dish and pour oil mixture over chicken. Secure openings with toothpicks. Bake uncovered in the oven for 30 to 35 minutes. Makes 4 servings.

Crunchy Cheese Sandwich

1 small onion, minced
1 medium tomato, diced
1 stalk celery, chopped
1 medium green bell pepper, finely chopped

1 C. shredded Cheddar cheese
¼ tsp. chili powder
¼ tsp. salt
4 slices white bread

Preheat the broiler to low. In a medium bowl, mix together the minced onion, diced tomato, chopped celery, minced bell pepper, shredded Cheddar cheese, chili powder and salt. Arrange slices of bread on a baking sheet. Top each slice with ¼ of the vegetable and cheese mixture. Broil for 4 to 5 minutes or until cheese melts. Do not let sandwiches burn. Serve sandwiches open-faced. Makes 4 servings.

Deep Fried Cheese Sandwich

1 qt. vegetable oil for frying
4 tsp. mayonnaise
4 slices white bread
4 slices Cheddar cheese

2 eggs
1 C. milk
2 C. dry bread crumbs

Heat oil in a deep-fryer to 365°. Spread 1 teaspoon of mayonnaise over each slice of bread. Place 2 slices of Cheddar cheese onto 1 slice of bread and place another slice of bread on top. Repeat with second sandwich. In a medium bowl, whisk together the eggs and milk. Place the dry bread crumbs in a medium shallow bowl. Dip each sandwich into the egg mixture, then into the bread crumbs and turn to coat. Immerse each sandwich, separately, into the deep-fryer. Fry each sandwich for 3 to 4 minutes or until the cheese is melted and the crust is golden brown. Place sandwiches on a paper towel to absorb excess oil before serving. Makes 2 servings.

Steak and Swiss Sandwich

1 tsp. butter
½ medium white onion, sliced
½ medium red onion, sliced
8 fresh mushrooms, sliced
1 clove garlic, minced
6 oz. beef sirloin, thinly sliced

¾ C. cream cheese, softened
1 tsp. Worcestershire sauce
Salt and pepper to taste
1 French baguette, cut in half lengthwise
½ C. shredded Swiss cheese

Preheat the broiler to low. In a large skillet over medium heat, melt butter. Sauté the sliced white onions, sliced red onions, sliced mushrooms and minced garlic in the butter until tender. Remove vegetables from the skillet and set aside. Place the sliced beef in the pan and fry for 5 minutes or until no longer pink. Reduce heat to low and stir in the cream cheese and Worcestershire sauce. Cook and stir until the beef is well coated; season with salt and pepper to taste. Place beef mixture on the bottom half of the French baguette and cover the beef with the onion mixture. Sprinkle shredded Swiss cheese over the onion mixture. Set open-faced sandwich along with top half next to it under broiler until the cheese is melted. Before serving, place top half of baguette on sandwich. Makes 1 to 2 servings.

Spinach Goat Cheese Turkey Burger

1½ lbs. ground turkey breast
1 C. frozen chopped spinach, thawed and drained
2 T. crumbled goat cheese
4 hamburger buns

Preheat the broiler to low. In a medium bowl, combine ground turkey, chopped spinach and crumbled goat cheese. Form the mixture into 4 patties. Arrange patties on a broiler pan and cook under the broiler for 5 to 7 minutes on each side or to desired doneness. To serve, place each patty on a bun. Makes 4 servings.

Blue Cheese Gravy and Pork Chops

2 T. butter
4 thick-cut pork chops
½ tsp. pepper
½ tsp. garlic powder
1 C. heavy cream
2 oz. blue cheese, crumbled

In a large skillet over medium heat, melt butter. Season the pork chops with pepper and garlic powder. Fry the pork chops in butter for 20 to 25 minutes until no longer pink and the juices run clear. Turn pork chops occasionally to brown evenly. Remove pork chops, set aside and keep warm. Stir heavy cream into the skillet and loosen pieces of meat stuck to the bottom of the skillet. Stir in the crumbled blue cheese. Cook for 5 minutes, stirring constantly until sauce thickens. To serve, pour sauce over warm pork chops. Makes 4 servings.

Feta Shrimp Pasta

3 T. olive oil, divided
1 lb. shrimp, peeled and deveined
5 cloves garlic, minced
1 T. white wine
1 (16 oz.) pkg. linguine
2 tomatoes, chopped
1 tsp. dried oregano
½ tsp. dried basil
1 (6 oz.) pkg. crumbled feta cheese
Parsley and additional grated Parmesan cheese, optional

In a medium skillet over medium heat, heat 2 tablespoons olive oil. Add shrimp, minced garlic and white wine; cook for 5 minutes or until shrimp is pink. Using a slotted spoon, remove shrimp and set aside. Bring a large pot of lightly salted water to a boil. Add linguine and cook for 8 to 10 minutes or until al dente. Drain water from pot and set aside. Add tomatoes, remaining 1 tablespoon olive oil, dried oregano and basil to white wine mixture. Cook for 10 minutes or until tomatoes are tender. Toss hot pasta with shrimp, tomato sauce and crumbled feta cheese. Allow feta cheese to melt slightly before serving. Makes 5 servings.

Chicken Cottage Cheese Enchiladas

- 1 T. vegetable oil
- 2 skinless, boneless chicken breast halves, boiled and shredded
- ½ C. chopped onion
- 1 (7 oz.) can chopped green chile peppers
- 1 (1 oz.) pkg. taco seasoning mix
- ½ C. sour cream
- 2 C. cottage cheese
- 1 tsp. salt
- Pinch of pepper
- 12 (6˝) corn tortillas
- 2 C. shredded Monterey Jack cheese
- 1 (10 oz.) can red enchilada sauce

Preheat the oven to 350°. In a medium skillet over medium heat, warm vegetable oil. Add shredded chicken, chopped onion and chopped green chile peppers. Cook until chicken is browned and vegetables are tender. Add taco seasoning and stir to coat. In a medium bowl, mix sour cream with cottage cheese. Season with salt and pepper; stir until well blended. Place tortillas on a microwave-safe plate and heat in microwave on medium power for 30 seconds or until tortillas are warm and soft. Place a spoonful of chicken mixture, a spoonful of cottage cheese mixture and some of the shredded Monterey Jack cheese in the center of each tortilla. Roll tortillas and place in a greased 9 x 13″ baking dish. Top with any remaining meat and cheese mixture, red enchilada sauce and remaining shredded Monterey Jack cheese. Bake in the oven for 30 minutes or until cheese is melted and bubbly. To serve, place 2 enchiladas on each individual dinner plate. Makes 6 servings.

Parmesan Beef and Garlic Pasta

1½ lbs. cubed beef steak
1 C. Italian seasoned bread crumbs
½ C. grated Parmesan cheese
2 T. olive oil
2 tsp. minced garlic, divided
1 medium onion, sliced into thin rings

1 medium green bell pepper, sliced into rings
1 (16 oz.) jar spaghetti sauce
½ C. shredded mozzarella cheese
1 (12 oz.) pkg. angel hair pasta
¼ C. butter

Preheat the oven to 350°. Cut cubed steak into smaller pieces. Combine bread crumbs and grated Parmesan cheese in a medium shallow bowl. Dip cubed steak pieces into bread crumb mixture and turn to coat. In a large skillet over medium heat, warm olive oil. Add 1 teaspoon of minced garlic and sauté for 3 minutes. Add cubed steak pieces to skillet and cook until browned on all sides. Place cubed steak pieces in a 2-quart baking dish. Top steak with onion rings and sliced green bell pepper and pour spaghetti sauce over top. Bake in the oven for 45 minutes or until meat is cooked throughout. Remove from oven and sprinkle shredded mozzarella cheese over meat. Return to oven and cook until cheese is melted and bubbly. Bring a large pot of lightly salted water to a boil. Add angel hair pasta and cook for 4 to 6 minutes or until al dente. Drain water from pot and toss in butter and remaining teaspoon of garlic. If desired, top pasta with parsley and additional grated Parmesan cheese for color. To serve, place a portion of cubed steak and sauce over a bed of angel hair pasta. Makes 4 servings.

Mushroom Mozzarella Chicken

3 T. olive oil
2 skinless boneless chicken breast halves
1 T. garlic powder
1 clove garlic, minced
6 fresh mushrooms, sliced
1 C. shredded mozzarella cheese

In a medium skillet over medium heat, warm olive oil. Place chicken breast halves in the skillet and season with garlic powder and minced garlic. Cook chicken for 12 minutes on each side or until juices run clear. Set chicken aside and keep warm. Stir sliced mushrooms into the skillet and cook until tender. Return chicken to skillet and layer with mushrooms. Top each chicken breast with ½ cup of shredded mozzarella cheese. Cover skillet and cook 5 minutes more or until cheese is melted. To serve, place each chicken breast on an individual dinner plate. Makes 2 servings.

Cheddar Bacon and Rice

5 slices bacon, diced
1 C. chopped onion
3 C. cooked rice
½ C. sliced olives
¼ C. whole pecans

Salt to taste
¼ tsp. pepper
2 C. cottage cheese
¾ C. shredded Cheddar cheese

Preheat the oven to 375°. In a medium skillet over medium heat, cook bacon and onion until bacon is browned and onion is tender. Drain grease from skillet. Add cooked rice, sliced olives, pecans, salt and pepper. Continue cooking until heated throughout. Remove skillet from heat and fold in the cottage cheese. Pour mixture into a greased 9 x 13" baking dish. Top with shredded Cheddar cheese. Bake in the oven for 15 to 20 minutes. To serve, spoon mixture onto individual dinner plates. Makes 6 servings.

Chicken Cordon Blue

6 skinless, boneless chicken breasts
6 slices Swiss cheese
6 slices ham

2 T. butter
1 (10.75 oz.) can cream of chicken soup
½ C. chicken broth

Preheat the oven to 350°. Pound the chicken breasts until flat. Place a slice of Swiss cheese and a slice of ham on each chicken breast. Roll up each chicken breast and secure with a toothpick. In a large skillet over medium-high heat, melt butter. Add chicken breast rolls and brown on all sides. Transfer chicken rolls to a 9 x 13" baking dish. In a medium bowl, combine cream of chicken soup and chicken broth. Pour mixture over chicken rolls. Bake in the oven for 20 minutes or until chicken is thoroughly cooked and sauce is bubbly. To serve, place each chicken roll on an individual dinner plate. Makes 6 servings.

Index

Appetizers

Asiago Cheese Toast	25
Baked Onion Spread	26
Blue Cheese Bread Bites	11
Blue Cheese Pizza	9
Blue Cheese Walnut Spread	21
Cheddar Cheesy Bacon Spread	24
Cheddar Olive Squares	8
Cheddar-Jack Cheese Bread	20
Cheesy Egg Salad Spread	7
Cheesy Sausage Balls	3
Four-Cheese Stuffed Bread	16
Garlic and Parmesan Zucchini Bites	4
Herbed Cheese Spread	19
Leek Tarts	13
Mini Ham and Cheese Quiches	15

Parmesan and Prosciutto Pinwheels 23
Parmesan Romano Bread 2
Pepperoni Provolone Pizza Swirls 14
Pesto and Parmesan Pita Wedges 1
Red Potato Nachos 18
Spicy Cheese Wafers 22
Stuffed Sausage Mushrooms 5
Sunshine Cheese Crisps 17
Swiss and Onion on Rye 10
Tortellini Bites 6
Two-Cheese Zucchini Squares 12

Breakfast and Brunch

American Egg Sandwich 40
Bagel and Cheese Bake 29
Cheese and Egg Puffs 42
Colby-Jack Breakfast Pizza 34
Crabby Cheddar Casserole 37
Feta Cheese Eggs 41

French Toast Surprise	36
Ham and Swiss Pie Casserole	39
Horseradish and Cheese Omelet	38
Mexican Egg Bake	28
Mozzarella Baked Omelet	31
Muenster Spinach Quiche	27
Sausage, Egg and Cheese Casserole	33
Swiss and Sausage Quiche	30
Three-Cheese Breakfast Bake	32
Vanilla Cheese Pancakes	35

Salads, Soups and Sides

Broccoli Cheese Soup	55
Cauliflower Cheese Soup	59
Cheddar Crabmeat Soup	62
Cheese Stuffed Potatoes	68
Cheesy Italian Taco Salad	43
Cheesy Potato Soup	53
Chèvre Green Bean Casserole	66

Chunky Cheese Soup	57
Cottage Cheese and Cucumber Salad	46
Easy Cheesy Pea Salad	48
Gorgonzola Salad	47
Green Tomatoes and Goat Cheese	74
Gruyère French Onion Soup	56
Layered Cheesy Macaroni	64
Leek, Potato and Mushroom Soup	58
Mozzarella Eggplant Au Gratin	69
Outback Onion Soup	60
Parmesan Baked Zucchini	65
Parmesan Garlic Broccoli	50
Pasta, Tomato and Mozzarella Salad	45
Red, White and Blue Cheese Slaw	49
Scrumptious Ricotta Stuffed Zucchini	72
Smoked Gouda and Salad Greens	51
Swiss Cheese Green Beans	70
Swiss Mushroom Salad	52
Three-Cheese Lettuce Salad	44

Three-Cheese Mashed Potatoes	63
Vegetable Cheese Soup	54
Warm Cheddar Corn	67
Wild Rice Soup	61
Zesty Pepper Jack Zucchini	71

Main Dishes

Blue Cheese Steak	76
Blue Cheese Gravy and Pork Chops	96
Blue Fettuccini Alfredo	83
Cheddar Apple Pork Chops	75
Cheddar Bacon and Rice	103
Cheddar Chicken Crescent Rolls	90
Cheddar Creole Chicken	80
Cheese Stuffed Lobster Tails	89
Cheesy Baked Ziti	78
Cheesy Chicken Pizza	85
Chicken Cordon Blue	104
Chicken Cottage Cheese Enchiladas	98

Crunchy Cheese Sandwich	92
Deep Fried Cheese Sandwich	93
Easy Cheesy Lasagna	87
Feta Shrimp Pasta	97
Feta Stuffed Chicken Breasts	91
Herbed Goat Cheese Salmon	88
Lasagna Roll-ups	79
Mozzarella Chicken Monte Cristo	81
Mushroom Mozzarella Chicken	102
Parmesan and Garlic Chicken Roll-ups	82
Parmesan Beef and Garlic Pasta	100
Pasta Cheese Pizza	86
Smoked Mozzarella Sandwich	84
Spinach Goat Cheese Turkey Burger	95
Steak and Swiss Sandwich	94
Three-Cheese Grilled Cheese	77